indoor
water features

indoor
water features

Philip Swindells

First edition for the United States and Canada
published in 2002 by Barron's Educational Series, Inc.
First published in 2002 by Interpet Publishing.
© Copyright 2002 by Interpet Publishing.

All inquiries should be addressed to:
Barron's Educational Series, Inc.
250 Wireless Boulevard
Hauppauge, NY 11788
www.barronseduc.com

International Standard Book No. 0-7641-1849-8
Library of Congress Catalog Card No. 2002105506

THE AUTHOR
Philip Swindells is a water gardening specialist with a
long experience of growing aquatic plants in many
parts of the world. He trained at the University of
Cambridge Botanic Garden and the famous aquatic
nursery of Perry's of Enfield, and ultimately became
Curator of Harlow Carr Botanical gardens, Harrogate.
The author of many publications on water gardening,
Philip was formerly the editor of *Water Garden
Journal* of the International Waterlily Society, who in
1994, inducted him into their Hall of Fame.

The information and recommendations in this book
are given without any guarantees on behalf of the
author and publisher, who disclaim any liability with
the use of this material.

Acknowledgments
The publisher would like to thank the following
people for their help during the preparation of this
book: "G" and Pat Kitchener at Old Barn Nurseries,
Dial Post, Horsham; Mike and Wendy Yendell of
Aristaquatics, Billinghurst; Stuart Thraves at Blagdon,
Bridgwater; Murrells Nursery, Pulborough, Gardens,
etc., Washington; Southdowns Ornaments for loan of
the fountain statue; and Belinda at Forest Lodge
Garden Centre, Farnham, for loan of a terrarium.

Printed in China
9 8 7 6 5 4 3 2 1

contents

introduction

The use of water in the home and garden for decorative purposes is one of the most popular recent innovations. With the advent of compact equipment, particularly submersible pumps, and the imaginative use of modern materials, water gardening in all its forms has become easy to try. This particularly applies to the use of water indoors.

Until recent years, water was rarely encountered inside the home as a decorative element. An occasional pool could be found in a conservatory adorned with a lotus or papyrus, or perhaps a tropical water lily, but other than that water was not commonly used. The growth in its popularity has resulted from the development of compact, self-contained moving water features. Tabletop and wall fountains are now available in garden centers in various styles and are used not only in the home but in the office and workplace as well.

The sound of moving water is therapeutic and the humidity that it provides is generally beneficial to the home environment. Aquatic plants can make a bold show, with the natives of the tropics being more exotic and sophisticated than their temperate counterparts, especially the deep-water and marginal species and varieties. Using an indoor water garden requires similar skills to successfully care for a traditional outdoor pool. However, light and temperature are more critical, because to maintain an all-year-round display of aquatics, the light

must be of high quality and the water temperature warm and consistent. Rather surprisingly, a number of usually terrestrial indoor plants adapt to aquatic cultivation, particularly those varieties that are usually grown as houseplants. This opens up a whole range of opportunities for the enthusiastic gardener, because although one or two species have been grown in aquariums for many years, a whole range of others are proving equally as versatile.

In addition to true water gardens, where a pool is the main component, planted aquariums offer the water gardener the chance to grow a wide range of aquatic plants indoors. Traditionally the preserve of the fishkeeper, these gardens can be transformed into leafy underwater landscapes and are especially valuable where space is limited. Not only can natural plantings be arranged but underwater "pictures" can be produced using both man-made and natural decorations.

Although terrariums and bottle gardens are on the fringe of aquaculture, they are often linked to it or become part of it. The same is true of insectivorous plant culture, which are naturally plants of swamps and marshes. If you want a decorative indoor water feature without a main component of plants or moving water, then consider a floating garden. Either with or without plants, the opportunities for enjoying water indoors are endless.

Above: A traditional-style wall fountain is easily installed and can successfully bring moving water indoors, without requiring too much space.
Right: Modern moving water features are more imaginative than ever, making use of the latest materials and technology.

raised conservatory pools

Water can add a new and exciting dimension to a conservatory. Not only can a wide range of interesting aquatic plants be cultivated, but the sound of moving water can be added to the ambience together with that delightful atmosphere that comes when water, plants, and warmth are grouped together.

The great benefit of a raised pool is that it can be easily added after the conservatory's construction – and because it is above ground level, it is easier to enjoy. Thoughtful design can ensure that provision is made for sitting on the edge of the pool and enjoying the fish and plants close up. There is nothing quite as therapeutic after a stressful day at work.

The addition of a fountain can change the whole feel of the conservatory, effectively serving as a humidifier and greatly improving the atmosphere for other plants. However, it does restrict the variety of plants that can

Below: *A large indoor pool can be planted like an outdoor pond with a reasonable expectation of achieving a natural ecobalance.*

Above: *A raised pool is easier to enjoy. The tiled edge allows you to sit and observe the fish and plants close up.*

Left: *Water does not have to be planted traditionally in order to be enjoyed. Here moving water falling into a small raised pool, without plants or fish, creates an attractive feature in a very modern setting.*

be used, because tropical water lilies, surface-floating aquatics and, to a lesser degree, lotus dislike moving water and do not prosper in its presence.

On the other hand, a fountain playing over an open water surface with an attractive spray pattern can be beautiful on its own. When illuminated from beneath with underwater lighting, it produces a magical effect. For the conservatory that is used essentially as extra living space, the moving water feature uncluttered by planting may be preferable.

indoor sunken pools

Creating a sunken pool indoors requires careful thought, especially when it is being constructed within an existing building rather than a new one. Removing the soil will cause considerable disruption, and creating a drainage system for the pool may cause problems if this is to be done using a method other than siphoning.

However, setting aside these considerations, a sunken indoor pool graced by tropical plants and alive with colorful fancy goldfish is a beautiful addition to any

building. Unlike a raised pool, a sunken pool does not create a visual obstruction in what is often a limited space. Apart from the labor of excavating the site, which can be considerable, such a pool can be constructed economically with a conventional pool liner being quite adequate in most cases.

Below: *Sunken pools contribute to the illusion of space, because they cause no visual obstruction. Here the plantings enhance the garden scene and protect the unwary who unexpectedly come upon the pool.*

Left: *This sunken pool creates an illusion of space and provides pleasing reflections. Such pools look particularly effective when the surrounding plants are lit from beneath.*

Below: *The secret of success with this pool is water clarity. Of all indoor pools, those holding clear water are surprisingly the most time-consuming to maintain.*

A sunken pool offers what is, perhaps, the most balanced environment of any indoor feature. Therefore provision should be made to add a variety of aquatic plants. Water lilies and lotus require deeper areas of water in which submerged aquatics also prosper. Marginal shelves or shallow areas for waterside and marginal aquatics is also essential. The technique of planting an indoor sunken pool is much the same as for an outdoor water garden, meaning that aquatic planting baskets and composts are essential if the plants are to be properly controlled and the pool easily maintained.

conservatory potted fountains

Although most newcomers to water gardening consider a fountain simply a jet of spray soaring heavenward or a tumbling liquid sculpture, in modern times it has taken on other forms, most popularly a small jet or bubbler in a pot.

Now very fashionable, these recent innovations have been brought about by the introduction of improved pumps in tiny sizes. Likely to be enduring features on the water gardening scene, they offer the gardener with very little indoor space a wonderful opportunity to enjoy moving water.

Above: *A simple bubbling water feature that can be used almost anywhere indoors to add sound and movement to a room.*

Right: *A potted fountain like this, where the submersible pump is positioned within the pot, must be topped off with water regularly.*

*ove: Large stones, colored pebbles, and ground glass are
nmonly used to dress the top of simple pot fountain arrangements that
not use plants as part of the decorative scheme.*

cause the pots are mostly quite small and the bubbling
spouting stream of water relatively strong, plants are
likely to prosper and may even be a nuisance in such
onfined space. Therefore it is better to use terrestrial
pical plants as an associated arrangement next to the
t.

Self-contained pot fountains with a built-in pump and a
nder electrical wire escaping from somewhere beneath
usually regarded more as tabletop features, although
ere are some fairly large, sophisticated creations

available, which may look more appropriate on the
floor of the conservatory.

The most impressive potted fountains are those that work
with a reservoir of water beneath them. Sometimes this
demands a small excavation before installation, although a
reservoir sited on the ground and disguised by surrounding
pots and plants to create an additional feature can
comfortably accommodate a potted fountain on top. In such
arrangements, a submersible pump sits in the reservoir and
the water is circulated up through the base of the pot.
Water tumbles over the edge of the pot onto a bed of gravel
or stones, these disguising the surface of the reservoir to
which the water returns by the action of gravity.

container water gardens

Container gardening is much in vogue and the wide range of modern materials that are available offer the gardener an enormous range of opportunities for colorful innovation. Although perennials, bulbs, bedding plants, and – to a limited extent – decorative shrubs have been used to great effect in containers, only recently have they been used for aquatic and bog gardens.

There is no reason why such plants should not be used in the same manner as bed and border plants. All that is required is a good aquatic planting compost as a growing medium and a water-tight container. Provided that sufficient room is allowed for topping off with water to create wetland conditions, the plants should be easy to cultivate.

Apart from the solitary pygmy water lily afloat in a small simple container, there are many opportunities for growing individual colorful aquatics and grouping them together in their containers. In a pond, they tend to grow quickly and swamp one another, especially in the confines of a small indoor pool. However, when properly planted and grown as large individual plants, they can grow unrestricted, yet at the same time be positioned in the most pleasing and readily changeable arrangement. Apart from decorative pots, aquatics can be successfully cultivated in more unusual containers and can even be used in window boxes.

Right: *The modern varieties of tropical arum lilies or callas are among the finest marginal plants for indoor cultivation. Types such as Zantedeschia 'Neroli' are perfect for growing as individual specimens in containers.*

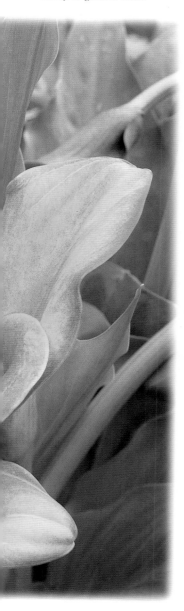

Right: *There are few finer plants than pygmy water lilies for individual cultivation in containers indoors in a conservatory or garden room.*

Right: *Although most container water gardens support an individual plant or small group of plants arranged neatly within them, they can be used in other ways. Here a small rugged pot with minimal aquatic planting provides a cool area of water in a colorful floral setting. In a well-planted conservatory, such a pool of water can also provide sustenance for the local fauna.*

water lilies and lotuses indoors

Among the many varieties of water lilies and lotuses, a number of them are well suited to indoor cultivation. Even if space is restricted, as long as the light is good and there is no water movement, they will prosper. It is important to choose with care, because many of the most spectacular varieties require plenty of room if they are to develop properly.

Choose from the many pygmy and dwarf varieties. With water lilies, you need not confine selection to truly tender kinds – some pygmy hardy varieties can be used as well. The canary yellow *Nymphaea* 'Pygmaea Helvola' and bright red *N.* 'Pygmaea Rubra' adapt well to indoor life and are especially pretty when grown in a small container. They will not tolerate tropical conditions, but a temperature between 72° and 82°F (22° and 28°C) will suit them well.

Although many lovely dwarf-growing tropical and sub-tropical water lilies, such as *N.* 'Daubenyana' and *N.* 'Margaret Mary,' will grow in higher temperatures if necessary, all must have plenty of light. Even night-blooming varieties must receive sufficient light during the day if they are to prosper.

The same applies to the smaller lotuses or *Nelumbo*. Although these are much more versatile than water lilies in that they will happily live in various depths of water from saturated compost up to 12 in (30 cm) of water, again adequate light is important.

Right: *Of all the tropical aquatics, it is the lotus or Nelumbo that catches the imagination of the indoor water gardener. Although it tolerates cold winter conditions outdoors in climates where the summers are long and hot, in most temperate conditions, the lotus is essentially an indoor plant and a priority for water gardeners. Many varieties are available, all easily grown indoors.*

Left: *Dwarf lotus are easily grown as individual plants in a pot or container. Their long banana-like tubers are planted in early spring, and by early summer the container is filled with circular leaves on short, stout, central stems. The beautiful blossoms in white, pink, or red are produced throughout the summer and last well into fall.*

Far left: *Tropical water lilies, like 'St. Louis Gold', are magnificent when grown as specimen plants in individual containers. Unlike their hardy counterparts, they are grown from tubers that can be removed and stored in a cool frost-free place in peat or sand for the winter. Many tropical water lilies have attractive foliage and are available in almost every color, including blue.*

illuminated features

The indoor water garden offers opportunities for the imaginative use of illumination. A controlled environment indoors allows you not only to create great effects using colored and moving lights but also to use candles without worrying that the wind will blow them out.

It may seem strange to associate candles with water, but some of the prettiest features use floating candles. Now widely available, these candles come in various shapes (including water lily shaped), colors, and scents. Floating

Right: *Illumination adds enormously to the enjoyment of an indoor water feature. Here the pool has been lit from below with white underwater lighting. Feature stones and plants have been highlighted with carefully positioned uplighters. It is important to make provision for such lighting during the planning and construction stages of the feature.*

Left: *The visual success this arrangement depen on the correct placeme of lights and the clever illumination of plants and water. Everything from the pots, plants, a water to the stones an painted wooden floori must be kept neat and minimalist for the ensemble to work successfully.*

Without artificial illumination, this simple, formal indoor [feat]ure would not look as bright and appealing as it does. [Car]eful lighting brings everything to life, highlighting the moving [wat]er from the wall fountain and the neatly manicured shrubs.

[Can]dles are ideal for an evening dinner party or similar [spec]ial occasion, because they produce an atmosphere that [is d]ifficult to achieve with electric lighting.

[C]onventional lighting can also be very effective. White [lig]hting is the most versatile, but subtle colors can be used [to] create special moods and themes. Soft blues and [ma]uves are particularly lovely. Lighting beneath the water [ca]n produce wonderful illusions, as can the use of carefully [po]sitioned mirrors to create reflections.

[U]nderwater electrical lighting is safe, provided that all [ins]tallation instructions are followed correctly. Modern [lig]hting systems use a transformer, which steps down the [vol]tage of the power, thus reducing the hazards of

combining electricity with water. Also, lighting units are so well sealed that problems are unlikely; however, caution is still necessary. What's more, waterproof connectors and circuit breakers or RCDs (residual current devices) that cut off the power supply in the event of a short circuit are vital.

small indoor fountains

When moving water is desired indoors and space is limited, wall fountains are the perfect solution. An individual wall fountain can be readily constructed from materials available at the garden center, or alternatively a custom-made wall fountain can be purchased, sited, and connected to the electrical supply.

Wall fountains are available in a wide range of configurations, but those that are purchased as self-contained units are made up of a reservoir and a small submersible pump, which circulates the water. Evaporation occurs quite readily, so the water should be topped off daily. Most aquatic plants dislike moving water, and given the limited opportunities for their cultivation within a wall fountain feature, they are usually excluded. However,

Above: A simple wall mask is a versatile indoor feature: It does not take up too much space yet it provides a generous flow of water.

Left: A group of bubblers can create a great effect. They operate from a submersible pump hidden in a reservoir beneath the gravel.

plants positioned around such a feature, usually growing in pots, can greatly enhance the overall effect.

Some wall fountains are also accompanied by a separate basal reservoir pool, the water being carried up through a pipe that is either chased into the plaster of the wall or threaded through the space in a cavity wall. An outlet is

created to spout from the wall mask or gargoyle and tumble into a pool below. A small group of marginal plants and, if the water is deep enough, a fancy goldfish or two can be added to the basal pool to create interest.

Apart from wall fountains, tabletop features are another option. These are usually self-contained fountains sited in a small bowl or container in which a miniature pump circulates water over decorative stones, shells, or colored

ght: *The regular symmetry of the wall*
ntain and the reservoir canal below
ables the water to be precisely
nneled.

ass chips. These are often dressed
th artificial foliage. Other styles of
ntainers, sporting copper leaves in
ascade arrangement or a series of
etallic scallops tumbling water from
e to the other, are also popular.
ese innovative decorative items are
nerally positioned as a focal point
a table or sideboard.

terrariums and bottle gardens

Terrariums and bottle gardens are like garden ponds in that they are almost self-sustaining environments. Large ponds, whether indoors or out, are capable of becoming completely balanced worlds where the various elements complement and depend on one another. With smaller ponds, however, the likelihood of total sustainability and successful interdependence diminishes.

This fact is also true of terrariums and bottle gardens, even where moisture-loving and wetland species are grown. The smaller the container, the less likely it is to be sustainable, but this need not detract from its beauty.

With a little ingenuity, this deficiency can be turned to advantage, by ignoring ecological balance and introducing strong visual elements.

Terrariums and bottle gardens are intended to reflect miniature tropical worlds. They are steamy swamp and jungle vignettes, glimpsed through a glass container or aquarium wall. The container itself can be as important as the tropical scene within. It can create a traditional

Below: *This bottle garden has an opening at one end, which permits air to circulate and reduces condensation.*

Victorian feel or an elaborate modern feel. The choice of plants is endless. By sidelining long-term sustainability and making the overall picture the priority, you can create a rich tropical atmosphere in no time at all.

Regular maintenance is important, especially where plants are crowded. Although a high level of moisture is required, excess water has no easy way to escape. Even plants from marshes and streamsides that traditionally thrive in moisture do not relish sitting in confined swampy conditions in a richly organic compost.

Above and left: *This terrarium and unusually shaped bottle garden show how beautifully a planted microcosm can be introduced into a conservatory or sunroom.*

23

aquariums for aquatic plants

Most people regard an aquarium as a setting for the enjoyment of decorative fish. The plants are a pleasing, but relatively unimportant element, except perhaps as a background or a source of food and cover for the fish. This lack of importance is reflected in the names that garden centers and aquatic suppliers use to describe them. Rarely are specific names used. Instead they are usually categorized under a collective name that can be as general as milfoils or pondweed. They are treated as a necessary, but much maligned, accessory. Fish, on the other hand, carry specific names, even down to individually colored fancy varieties.

Below: Aquarium plants are often overlooked when an indoor water feature is considered. However, aquariums are not just for fish: Beautiful plants can be used where no fish are present.

With the growing popularity of smaller water features and innovative indoor aquatic creations, the role of aquariums is being reviewed and aquarium plants afforded more attention. Among the wealth of submerged subtropical and tropical aquatics, some species and varieties can coexist happily together in aquariums where the occasional fish can be tolerated but the underwater picture is predominantly created by plants.

Many wonderful aquarium plants are available, including individual varieties that are so eye-catching that they can turn the head of even the most sceptical interior artist. The marvellous Madagascar lace plant, *Aponogeton fenestralis,* with its latticework leaves is spectacular when backlit in an aquarium. What's more, the richly colored foliage of the trumpet plants, or *Cryptocorynes,* and the striking leaves of the *Alternanthera* produce an underwater tropical extravaganza that is difficult to surpass.

Left: As with the outdoor pool where fish and plants live harmoniously together and create a balanced ecosystem, so a similar happy arrangement can be achieved indoors. This is a contained world where plants, fish, and other aquatic creatures live together, each depending on the other for their continued existence. In such an arrangement, the plants play a key role, the fish being added sparingly once the plants have become established.

indoor aquascapes

Although submerging tropical aquatic plants in an aquarium uncluttered by fish produces a pleasing leafy and tropical focal point in the home or conservatory, creating an aquascape takes things a step further by producing an underwater picture or tableau.

Garden centers and aquatic shops now sell various ornaments for the aquarium, from sunken castles and goldfish bowls to elaborate colonnades and statuary to colored rocks and coral to colorful dioramas that can be attached to the back wall of the tank for an instant effect. There are as many opportunities in the aquarium for creating an appealing aquascape as there are in the garden for producing a beautiful landscape.

right: An all-glass
*aquarium shows an
aquascape off to full
advantage.*

below: A beautifully
*designed aquarium,
arranged as a true
aquascape with
submerged, floating,
and marginal plants,
provides a focal point
for any room.*

Although many purists prefer to arrange natural materials such as rocks, stones, and bog oak with associated plantings, freethinkers use other materials to produce a rich diversity of aquascapes, from miniature sunken worlds to outlandish modern designs.

There are no rules where aquascapes are concerned, unless plants are to form an important part of the arrangement, in which case a suitable growing medium and adequate light are needed. If fish are to be introduced, then no artifacts that could pollute the water should be included. The most harmful of these is copper, which, although beautiful, can be toxic to fish and lead to their death. Otherwise, the boundaries for exciting and innovative creations are restricted only by the imagination of the aquascape's creator.

pumps and equipment

Most indoor water gardens depend on a pump for their success – and the modern submersible pump has really revolutionized things. Nowadays submersible pumps are so neat and compact that they take up little room and only need connection to the electrical supply to be fully functional.

A submersible pump is essential for creating a feature that incorporates moving water. The pump can also be connected to a simple filtration system in an indoor pool. With an aquarium, other options are available. An air pump may be used to operate the filtration system and the pump may be situated outside the tank. Either system works well for filtering debris from the water, the air pump also being a primary supplier of air to oxygenate the water, which is important when many fish are present.

The selection of a submersible pump for an indoor water garden should depend primarily on the flow of water required and then on its size and configuration. The latter is important if the water garden is modestly sized, although with the tiniest tabletop water gardens, it is common for a small pump to be integrated into the container itself.

Filtration systems vary from a simple attachment to a pump that takes larger suspended debris from the water to undergravel filters that occupy the entire floor of the aquarium beneath the gravel and work on a biological system whereby the debris that the fish excrete is trapped and broken down naturally by colonies of beneficial bacteria.

An Aquarium Filter

This compact pump and filtration system fits neatly into the corner of an aquarium. Water is drawn into the filter body and aquatic debris captured in the filter sponge. A filtration system such as this is essential for an aquarium that is populated with fish, but it is unnecessary for an aquascape that consists entirely of plants. The filter body and sponge should be taken apart and cleaned regularly.

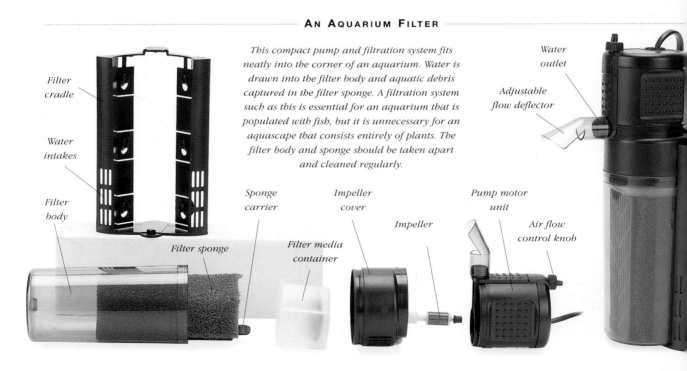

Filter cradle

Water intakes

Filter body

Filter sponge

Sponge carrier

Filter media container

Impeller cover

Impeller

Pump motor unit

Air flow control knob

Water outlet

Adjustable flow deflector

Above: *When selecting a pump, make sure that it is powerful enough to lift the required volume of water to the required height.*

Left: *Fogger units are extremely useful for creating a mysterious effect. Keep in mind, however, they do splash.*

Right: *Components such as these help to bring indoor water features to life.*

Fogger unit

Combined pump and light

Submersible pump

plants for indoor features

Many decorative aquatic plants are available for the indoor water garden, from tropical water lilies and lotuses to arum lilies and water hyacinths. Each has much to offer, although space limitations usually mean that they cannot be grown in such diversity as hardy aquatics in an outdoor pool. Most indoor pools are much smaller than their outdoor equivalents, and other water features have space limitations, which means that only selected specimens can be grown if the best effect is to be achieved.

Water lilies are a natural choice, not only the more restrained tropical species and varieties but also the hardy pygmy kinds, which are also well suited to indoor cultivation. Lotuses are also a good choice, particularly the pygmy and rice bowl varieties. Although all can be grown as part of a general

pool planting, they are best cultivated individually in attractive containers and then arranged together in visual harmony.

Marginal and bog garden plants are numerous, and many varieties, such as the callas and arum lilies and members of the *Cyperus* species are commonly grown as houseplants. When introduced to truly aquatic conditions in containers they often produce a more striking display.

Submerged plants are dominated by those popularly grown in cold-water or tropical aquariums. Although many are genuine submerged aquatic plants that can only be cultivated in this manner, many popular foliage houseplants can be completely submerged if they are planted when they are young. An illustration of such a planting is shown on pages 56-57.

Many different tropical plants are available for use with indoor water gardens. Most garden centers offer a wide range year-round.

Selaginella

Asplenium *species*

Pilea cadierei

Fittonia 'Purple Anne'

Polypodium *species*

Calceolaria *hybrid*

Helxine soleirolii

Cyperus
diffusus

Guzmania
lingulata

Spathiphyllum *hybrid*

Scindapsus
variegatus

Dieffenbachia
exotica

Chamaedorea
elegans

*Many traditional houseplants can
readily adapt themselves to various roles
in an indoor water feature.*

Left: *Aquarium
plants need feeding.
Use a soluble plant
food for aquatic
plants, which absorb
minerals through
their leaf surfaces.
Other rooted plants
benefit from slow-
release fertilizer
added to the soil.*

*Lotus and tropical water lilies are among the most colorful
aquatic plants:* Nelumbo lutea *and* Nymphaea *'King of the Blues.'*

installing a conservatory pool and fountain

A conservatory pool offers a great opportunity for growing a range of interesting tropical and subtropical aquatic plants. If you plan to include a fountain, it is generally not advisable to include aquatic plants in the setup, but a pleasing arrangement of indoor plants can be used around the pool to enhance the overall look and ambience. The addition of moving water creates a pleasing humid atmosphere and provides both relaxing sounds and movement. Various ornamental fountains – from classical nymphs to modern metal obelisks – are readily available at garden centers nowadays.

Although a conservatory pool is constructed indoors, the requirements are similar to those for the outdoor water garden. They should, however, be modified according to what is practical and desired. A number of patio pools are now available in "flat pack" form, which any competent do-it-yourself enthusiast can construct at home. These are particularly appropriate for use inside a conservatory. Most come with a robust plastic reservoir pool, which is concealed by a decorative wooden surround.

If plants are to be used either in or as a background to the conservatory pool, then adequate light is essential. Spring temperatures are often disproportionately high when compared with the quality of light available and elongated plant growth results. So ensure the best possible light conditions for your plants from the outset.

PREFABRICATED POOL CONSTRUCTION

1 *Before assembly, paint the prefabricated wooden sections that contain the pool with a suitable preservative. Various color shades are available.*

2 *Screw together each section, both top and bottom. Make sure that all screws are used and that each section is aligned accurately with the next to guarantee a secure structure.*

3 *When half of the structure has been completed, insert the inner pool section. The timber lips that form both the top and the bottom of the framework secure the pool neatly within.*

4 *With the pool complete, provision can be made for a fountain. A level plinth is necessary. The best way to achieve this is by using two three layers of clean bricks*

Insert the pump outflow tube into the ornament, and seal it so it is secure. Many of the waterproof sealants available today do ensure a firm bond.

6 With the ornament in position, connect the pump and place it on the pool floor.

Greenery is best provided as an accompaniment to a fountain feature because few true aquatic plants tolerate moving water in such a confined space.

STONE RAISED POOLS

Left: *This small pool also allows other indoor plants to be enjoyed in its proximity. Although they benefit from the humidity that the water provides, they do create an obstacle to easy pool maintenance.*

Right: *The planters that are incorporated into the structure of this pool wall are independent of the pool itself, but they could be linked to it if so desired.*

bamboo spout fountain

The oriental look is very fashionable now, and bamboo helps create that look when used with simple glazed pottery to make a fountain. Bamboo canes can be used as pipes to carry water if the dividing sections between the solid leaf nodes or joints are cut or drilled through to permit the water to flow along the length of the bamboo cane, and a wide range of these canes are available. In many cases, the distances between the leaf joints are long enough that you can establish a suitable spout without drilling.

You can create an attractive simple indoor feature by taking a length of bamboo and splicing in a smaller bamboo spout. The spout should be of sufficient diameter to accommodate a narrow flexible tube that will be attached to a submersible pump. The tube leads from the pump, up through the larger diameter section of bamboo,

and fits neatly into the spout. It is ideal if the tube and spout are of roughly the same diameter; however, the tube can be glued into the spout with sealant without it showing if necessary.

The upright pipe should be sited vertically next to the small submersible pump and wedged into the pot with large stones. The pump sits neatly on the floor of the pot with large stones placed around it so that a small chamber is created. More stones are added, followed by a decorative top layer of pebbles. Enough water is then poured into the pot so that the pump is completely submerged. The pump circulates the water up through the bamboo, out of the spout, and back into the pot in a circular flow. Evaporation will lower the water level over time, so check regularly to see if the water needs topping off.

MAKING A BAMBOO SPOUT FOUNTAIN

1 *Select two suitable short lengths of bamboo of different diameters. Cut the smaller diameter length to form a lip at one end and drill a hole through the large section toward the top end so that the shorter length can be inserted into it to form a spout.*

2 *Thread the flexible outflow tube from the pump through the newly drilled hole and down into the bamboo up-pipe. If the old leaf joint or node within the bamboo forms a solid obstruction, drill this out to allow the tube to pass through and be connected to the pump.*

3 *Glue the short length of bamboo, which is to serve as the spout, into the main upright bamboo, threading the outflow tube inside. Seal the joint with sealant.*

Position the bamboo upright in the pot using ... or three large stones to wedge it in place. ...ke sure the outflow tube is not pinched.

5 Place the pump on the bottom of the pot, and connect it to the outflow tube that runs up inside the bamboo.

6 Position a wire support next to the bamboo upright. This wedges into the pot about two-thirds of the way up.

Below: Here the water flows over the pot and through the stones into a reservoir below.

Place several large polished stones ... the wire support, both to disguise it ...d to create a water chamber for the ...np below. Then fill the pot with ...er to just beneath the level of the ...nes.

Left: The finished fountain will need regular topping off.

creating an aquatic plant display

One of the best ways of growing tropical and subtropical aquatic and marginal plants is in decorative pots. Although theoretically they should grow best in a traditional latticework aquatic planting basket in aquatic compost, this is only the case in a warm tropical or subtropical climate when they are out in the open.

In a conservatory or outdoor room, the conditions are not always conducive to successful growth in static water features because light and temperature often vary. When plants are grown in pots, however, they can be easily moved around to take advantage of suitable conditions.

Marginal aquatics are particularly well suited to being grown individually in pots, and once well established they make a striking feature. Carefully select the pot – it must be both of sufficient size to accommodate the plant and of an appearance that complements it. Growing a large papyrus in an Arabian-looking pot or a *canna* in a hot-colored container to reflect the plant's Indian origin can make all the difference to the overall effect of the planting.

Plants can be grown in pots of the same design, but of varying dimensions, and grouped together for a pleasing effect. Alternatively, if your pots are simply functional and have no intrinsic beauty, then set the arrangement within a larger decorative feature.

Regardless of the arrangement, all tropical and subtropical marginal plants should be grown in an aquatic planting compost and set sufficiently low in the pot so that a couple inches of water can be maintained over the compost surface.

PLANTING A DECORATIVE POT

1 *Many decorative pots are suitable for cultivating aquatics. Most have drainage holes, which require sealing. The simplest method of making a pot watertight involves putting waterproof sealant in the hole and embedding a marble into it.*

2 *Place a generous layer of aquatic planting compost into the bottom of the pot. The new plant will root strongly into this.*

3 *Remove the plant from its pot, and place it in position. Make sure the top of the rootball is several inches below the top of the pot to allow for additional water.*

Plants Used
Cyperus papyrus/year-round/marginal
Canna hybrids/summer/marginal
Zantedeschia (Calla) **hybrids**/summer and
    fall/marginal

Alternative Plants
Cyperus alternifolius/year-round/
    marginal
Thalia dealbata/summer/marginal

Below: *Fine examples of subtropical
marginal aquatics that adapt readily to
container cultivation.* **From left to right:**
Zantedeschia *hybrid,* Cyperus
papyrus, *and* Canna *hybrid.*

4 *Once more compost has been added and*
rmed down, coat the surface with a layer
well-washed gravel.

5 *Saturate the compost with water. When*
potting is complete, the plant should be
standing in several inches of water.

*This wall fountain uses a spider plant, or Chlorophytum,
for decoration. Although not an aquatic plant, it is
growing in a sealed pot plunged in the water. Regular
repotting is necessary.*

planting a window box for bog plants

Window boxes are traditionally positioned beneath a window, suspended on brackets and filled with colorful annuals, biennials, bulbs, or herbs. They use a lightweight compost and are usually replanted twice a year. In recent years, however, there have been changes in conventional thinking about the window box, not only regarding the plants it might accommodate but also its role in the garden. What was once regarded simply as a window box is now considered a versatile trough, commonly filled with perennials.

This trend has resulted in the manufacturing of a wide array of window boxes and troughs that can accommodate any kind of plant that the imaginative gardener may care to grow. Many of them are actually too big to successfully fulfill their original function of providing color at the

Right: *The popular arum or calla lilies are ideal for window box cultivation.* Zantedeschia *'Rubilite Rose' is one of a modern generation of varieties that are widely available from garden centers.*

PLANTING A BOG WINDOW BOX

···· PLANTING SUGGESTIONS ····

Plants Used

Chamaedorea elegans/year-round/bog
Cyperus diffusus/year-round/bog
Dieffenbachia exotica/year-round/bog
Guzmania lingulata/summer and fall/ bog
Scindapsus variegatus/year-round/bog
Spathiphyllum hybrid/year-round/bog

Alternative Plants

Acorus gramineus 'Variegatus'/year- round/bog
Zantedeschia (Calla) hybrids/summer and fall/bog

1 *Make sure any drainage holes in the window box are sealed. Place a layer of gravel in the bottom to a depth of about 1 inch (2.5 cm), and then add aquatic planting compost.*

2 *If an epiphytic moisture-loving plant, su as a bromeliad, is to be introduced, a spec pocket of peaty organic compost is needed, however, it should not be be saturated.*

With a bromeliad like Guzmania, *it is sier to manage composting and watering if s planted to one end.*

4 *Close planting for instant effect is acceptable, because the plants are not allowed to reach maturity. Regular dividing is essential.*

5 *Once the planting is complete, spread a layer of well-washed gravel over the compost for a decorative finish.*

Water thoroughly to settle the compost. gular watering should ensure that the window x is constantly moist but not waterlogged.

7 *As bog plants benefit from establishment in a soil-based aquatic compost, a planted window box is more often used as a trough because of its weight. A densely planted arrangement will require regular manicuring and periodic replanting in order to keep it fresh and vibrant.*

ndow ledge, but nevertheless they can make an portant contribution to the garden.

With careful selection, it is possible to produce an ractive bog garden in a window box. However, unless s placed on a substantial window ledge, the box could t be sited beneath a window, because the saturated

aquatic planting compost would make it too heavy. However, used more as a trough it can be both versatile and attractive, and it can be easily maintained within a conservatory or other indoor setting.

growing a pygmy water lily in a bowl

Pygmy water lilies are wonderful indoor plants. Although most are completely hardy, they adapt well to subtropical conditions and are completely at home in a small bowl in the conservatory or living room. Grown alone, few other decorative aquatic plants are as attractive as pygmy water lilies.

All are easy to cultivate, requiring a generous layer of aquatic planting compost on the bottom of the pot and a liberal sprinkling of well-washed gravel over the surface to prevent the compost from escaping into the water.

Water is then poured in, and during the growing season it should be regularly topped off to maintain a level near the rim of the pot. Apart from occasionally removing any filamentous algae that appears and regularly dead-heading and de-leafing of faded blossoms and foliage, the pot-grown pygmy water lily is almost entirely self-sustaining.

Of the hardy varieties, the best and most free-flowering is *Nymphaea* 'Pygmaea Helvola.' This beautiful canary-yellow-flowered variety has dark olive-green leaves that are splashed with maroon and chocolate flecks.

PLANTING A PYGMY WATER LILY

1 *Spread aquatic planting compost directly on the bottom of the bowl. As much as one-third of the depth of the bowl can be filled with compost.*

2 *Plant the water lily in the compost in the center of the bowl with just the nose of the crown above compost level. Water the compost in the bowl thoroughly.*

3 *Cover the surf of the compost evenly wi thin layer of well-washed gravel. This helps to preve compost escaping and discoloring the water.*

4 *Add water, taking care not to disturb the gravel. Pour it gently onto a square of polyethelene. Arrange the water lily foliage evenly over the surface of the water.*

Right: *A pygmy water lily makes a wonderful centerpiece for a decorative bowl. When grown indoors such water lilies blossom freely for most of the summer.*

'ygmaea Rubra' is an excellent red
pe, although others do flower
ore. 'Pygmaea Alba' is the tiniest
hite-flowered water lily. 'Joanne
ring' is pink and not as hardy as the
thers. 'Daubenyana' is subtropical
ith blue flowers.

All dwarf and pygmy water lilies
ower in the summer. As fall
proaches and their foliage naturally
des, water can be removed from the
owl and the plants dried off.

*Above: Gardeners who wish to grow a
pygmy water lily in a large bowl or
container may find it easier to grow the
plant in a proper aquatic planting basket. A
small basket enables the plant to be controlled
more easily, because the basket can be lifted
out for division, repotting, or feeding.*

Provided that the compost does not
completely dry out, water can be
added the following spring and they
will return to life, although it is wise
to replace their compost annually.

···· PLANTING SUGGESTIONS ····

Plants Used
Nymphaea 'Pygmaea Helvola'/ summer/
  aquatic

Alternative Plants
Nymphaea 'Daubenyana'/summer/aquatic
Nymphaea 'Joanne Pring'/summer/aquatic
Nymphaea 'Pygmaea Alba'/summer
  aquatic
Nymphaea 'Pygmaea Rubra'/summer/
  aquatic

planting a bottle garden

Planting a bottle garden is a practical way to produce a suitable environment for cultivating a range of attractive tropical plants, including moisture-loving and bog garden subjects. What's more the bottle part does not necessarily have to be the traditional carboy, which is a giant spherical bottle originally intended for the transporting of chemicals. It can be of any shape or size, provided the plants have room to develop and you a means of gaining access for planting and maintenance.

The glass from which the bottle is made should be clear and unblemished, although a green, bronze, or blue bottle can enhance the overall appearance without unduly affecting plant performance. Positioning is important, because although plenty of light is required for the plants to prosper, a bottle garden can become extremely hot if positioned in a sunny window.

Because a bottle garden is not self-sustaining, planting can be more intensive than if a natural environment were being created. However, this does mean that the garden requires more maintenance if everything is to be kept in good order, and plants will need to be replaced as they fade and die.

PLANTING A BOTTLE GARDEN

1 *Use a soil-based potting compost if available. Pour this through a funnel made of rolled-up cardboard or newspaper. This helps to prevent dirtying the sides of the bottle. Spread a drainage layer of gravel over the floor of the bottle.*

Gravel

Compost

2 *Spread the compost evenly over the gravel. View it from the outside to make sure it is completely level.*

3 *Take the centerpiece plant, in this case Selaginella martensii, and plant it in the center of the bottle. Firm gently into the compost.*

Plant the secondary plants, but make sure they have some room to develop. Create as pleasing an arrangement as possible.

For a more polished look, topdress the compost with gravel, chips, or colored shell fragments. Remember to water frequently.

colored shell fragments

Above: *This bottle garden has been stoppered so that a completely self-contained ecosystem might be established. The drawback to this is the regular flow of condensation down the inside of the glass, which can obscure the attractive planting.*

PLANTING SUGGESTIONS

Plants Used

Asplenium spp./year-round/houseplant
Calceolaria hybrids/summer/houseplant
Fittonia 'Purple Anne'/year-round/
  houseplant
Helxine soleirolii/year-round/
  houseplant
Pilea cadierei/year-round/houseplant
Selaginella martensii/year-round/
  houseplant

Alternative Plants

Hypoestes sanguinolenta/year-round/
  houseplant
Ficus pumila/year-round/houseplant

creating a floating candle garden

Attractive indoor water gardens do not have to accommodate aquatic plants or moving water, nor do they have to be long lasting. Pleasing arrangements can be made for dinner parties and similar social events, using water as the medium and a range of natural materials, such as dried fruits and seed pods, floating on the surface of a bowl of water. Candles are now available in wide array of styles and designs, and some are even made to float gently on the surface of the water. Many candles are aromatic, releasing an attractive combination of flickering light and fragrant perfume as they burn.

Although any suitable container can be used, one that is shallow and has a large surface area is preferable. Just make sure it is cleaned thoroughly before you use it in an arrangement. If a plant is to be used as a centerpiece, such as the grassy *Scirpus cernuus*, then make sure the container is deep enough to accommodate the plant pot or basket in which it is growing. A small growing plant is especially useful in a floating arrangement because lends height and visual stability.

Most floating arrangements have a short life and need to be replaced regularly. What's more, there is always the danger of organic material starting to decompose and pollute the water. However, using dried materials greatly reduces this risk, especially if the water is changed regular Remember when using candles that they do pose a fire hazard if left unattended – so use them safely, and make sure if you are using a plant as a centerpiece that you raise it high enough from the surface of the water so it doesn't get scorched by the candle flames.

PLANTING SUGGESTIONS

Plant Used
Scirpus cernuus/year-round/marginal

Alternative Plants
Cyperus alternifolius 'Nanus'/year-round/marginal
Zantedeschia (Calla) 'Godfrey'/summer and autumn/marginal

Left: *A wonderful table centerpiece for the evening. It is important to take heed of the dangers of candle flames, especially if they are close to plants. After an evening of enjoyment, it will be necessary to empty the water out and refill the bowl. If any wax has melted into the water, an oily, unsightly scum will coat the surface.*

MAKING A TABLE CENTERPIECE WITH CANDLES

3 *The* Scirpus cernuus *centerpiece plant can be purchased growing through a tube like this. Tease out the tangled foliage, and then cover the surface of the pot with a layer of well-washed gravel.*

Remove the stem and the base of the lotus d pods neatly with a pair of scissors so t they float evenly.

2 *To add a touch of color and sophistication, decorate the seed pods with gold or silver spray paint. Allow the paint to dry thoroughly.*

4 *Invert a clean plant pot into the center of the bowl. Place the plant in position on top of it, and then add the water.*

Finish off with lighted floating candles.

Place the lotus seed pods evenly around the nt, and add other decorative natural materials.

making a tabletop fountain

A tabletop fountain is an attractive centerpiece for a table or sideboard. However, because moving water is involved, a pump and an electrical connection must be incorporated. This will involve a trailing cable, which may be more easily disguised if the fountain is positioned on a sideboard. Remember also that such features can create splashes, so be careful where you site it – after all, it is easy to damage polished or veneered wooden surfaces.

A tabletop fountain is usually constructed inside a bowl or container that houses a small submersible pump. The electrical lead for this is generally passed through a hole in the base of the container and securely sealed with silicone sealant. Alternatively, the head can be draped over the back of the container and hidden by the display itself. The pump rests on the bottom of the container and may be protected in a small chamber, made up of an inverted plant pot or merely surrounded by substantial stones.

The container is filled with water to within a few inches of the top, and then a fountain head is contrived to spout water onto a decorative feature or bubble out of the level surface of a stone as illustrated. The pipe that conducts the water is normally made of clear flexible tubing that is the right diameter to slip securely onto the outlet pipe of the pump. If necessary, it can be fixed securely with silicone sealant. It is important to fill the container with

CREATING A TABLETOP FOUNTAIN

1 *Seal the drainage holes in the base of the pot using a waterproof sealant. Allow it to dry for several hours.*

2 *Drill a hole through a flat stone, and pass into it the outlet tube from the pump. Suitable pre-drilled stones are available from many garden centers. Unless the tube fits tightly, it is best sealed in place.*

3 *Put the submersible pump in place, and carefully add decorative stones. The spaces between the stones will form chamber or reservoir for the pump.*

4 *Position the centerpiece stone carefully. Add water, and run the pump so that the flow can be fine-tuned.*

5 *Add plants in their pots. Provided the they are not sitting in water, they need not be true aquatics.*

Once the bowl is topped with water, the fountain *ready to be switched on. *b a tabletop fountain *his kind, remember that *an be used on a dresser or *eboard where the electrical wire *n be hidden from view.

Above right: A little extra glamour can be added in the evening with a lighted candle. Take care not to position it too closely to the plants. Use a fragrant candle for sensuous enjoyment.

ter and to run the pump before all decorative stones are aced in position, because it may require some adjusting ensure that the flow of water is even over the stones. e final coating of decorative stones and pebbles is then plied.

Tabletop fountains come in many forms. Tiny pumps are adily available, and they simply need to be positioned in suitable containers filled with rocks, shells, pebbles, and glass chips in varying configurations to create an attractive feature. The nice thing about these fountains is you can change its components regularly, as the seasons change or as the mood takes you. The addition of small moisture-loving plants also helps to bring a feature to life and to soften its contours.

planting a terrarium

A terrarium is like a small garden created within a greenhouse. The Wardian case of Victorian times, which was used to transport rare and unusual plants from far-flung corners of the globe, is typical of the kind of structure that may be used to create a traditional terrarium.

Although many terrariums feature liberal plantings of a wide range of subtropical plants, small reptiles, and other exotic creatures, some of the finest terrariums embrace those plants that naturally inhabit moist places. A terrarium can create a humid atmosphere as well as offer damp soil conditions for moisture-loving subtropical plants.

Although the plants that grow best in a terrarium are moisture-loving plants, they do not benefit from saturated compost conditions. Constant moisture is much to be preferred. Thoroughly wet compost leads to rotting, rapid deterioration of organic matter, and population by sciarid flies.

Unlike an aquarium or a bottle garden, where plants are typically crowded together for effect and frequent maintenance is necessary, the best terrariums are usually sparingly planted and the plants permitted to grow and develop naturally in the space available to them, much like traditional indoor plants in a conservatory.

PLANTING A TERRARIUM

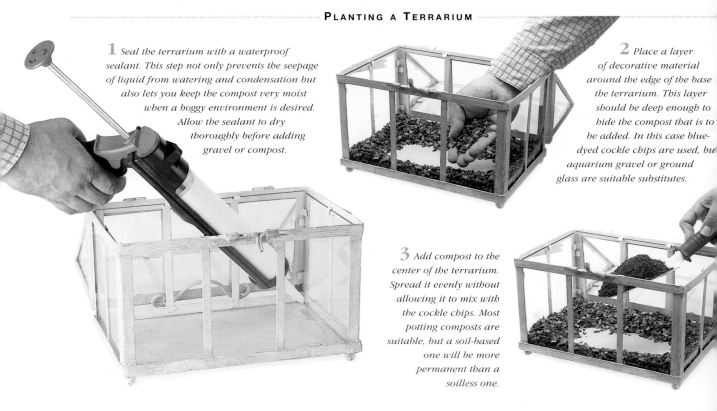

1 *Seal the terrarium with a waterproof sealant. This step not only prevents the seepage of liquid from watering and condensation but also lets you keep the compost very moist when a boggy environment is desired. Allow the sealant to dry thoroughly before adding gravel or compost.*

2 *Place a layer of decorative material around the edge of the base the terrarium. This layer should be deep enough to hide the compost that is to be added. In this case blue-dyed cockle chips are used, but aquarium gravel or ground glass are suitable substitutes.*

3 *Add compost to the center of the terrarium. Spread it evenly without allowing it to mix with the cockle chips. Most potting composts are suitable, but a soil-based one will be more permanent than a soilless one.*

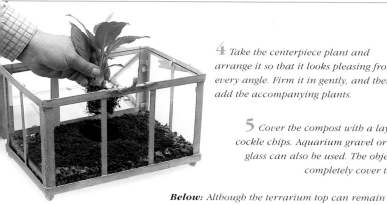

4 *Take the centerpiece plant and arrange it so that it looks pleasing from every angle. Firm it in gently, and then add the accompanying plants.*

5 *Cover the compost with a layer of cockle chips. Aquarium gravel or ground glass can also be used. The objective is to completely cover the compost.*

Below: *Although the terrarium top can remain closed to produce a humid atmosphere, the top can also be raised to reduce condensation and allow air to circulate.*

Water the plants gently from overhead ...ng a watering can with a fine rose. ...errarium will require watering only ...aringly after it's initially established.

PLANTING SUGGESTIONS

Plants Used

Codiaeum (Croton) variegatus/year-round/houseplant

Hypoestes hybrid/year-round/houseplant

Pilea cadierei/year-round/houseplant

Spathiphyllum hybrid (dwarf form)/year-round/houseplant

Alternative Plants

Helxine soleirolii/year-round/houseplant

Selaginella martensii 'Aurea'/year-round/houseplant

making an insectivorous plant swamp garden

Most insectivorous plants originate from swampy areas. Some are epiphytic and cling to moss and debris in the crooks of the branches, but the most commonly cultivated species and varieties are native to terrestrial swamps, usually flourishing in peaty or mossy locations.

Insectivorous plants developed the ability to capture and digest insects partly because of the poor growing conditions they have to endure. A wet mossy environment is naturally deficient in many of the nutrients that plants require. Insectivorous plants correct this by capturing and ingesting insects, which yield up the various minerals of which their growing medium is deficient.

When making an insectivorous plant swamp garden, it is essential that a poor growing medium be used – ideally one of raw peat mixed with chopped live sphagnum moss, the same moss that is popularly sold for hanging baskets. This produces open but wet growing conditions, which are perfect for insectivorous plants like *Sarracenia, Darlingtonia,* and *Dionaea,* or Venus's flytrap.

In addition to a damp growing medium, most insectivorous species enjoy a humid atmosphere. To achieve this, you can use a clear cover like the one illustrated here, provided that excessive condensation can be controlled. You can also use vents in the lid of the propagation tray to prevent excessive humidity from building up.

Above: *Venus's flytrap,* Dionaea muscipula, *is the best-known insectivorous plant. I captures and digests insects in its traps in order to correct nutritional deficiencies.*

MAKING A SWAMP GARDEN

Sphagnum moss   Soilless compost

1 *The best ingredients for a compost mixture are fresh green sphagnum moss and soilless compost, especially low-nutrient seed or cutting compost.*

2 *Chop up the green sphagnum moss, add enough volume soilless compost to increase the mixture by about half, and mix thoroughly by hand.*

Seal any drainage holes, and then place
compost mixture into the watertight tray
a small propagator, spreading it out to
most the depth of the tray.

4 *Take the principal plant – here* Sarracenia
*is used – and position it carefully. If the root
ball is too deep for the tray, remove some
compost from the bottom.*

5 *Arrange the other insectivorous plants
so that there is a little space between them
and they are not touching. Tamp down the
compost around the plants.*

7 *Water the plants
thoroughly using a
watering can with a fine
rose. Replace the lid. For a
closed environment shut
the ventilators on the top.*

8 *Once established, the
garden is sustainable,
especially if the moss starts to
grow. Although opportunities for
capturing insects are limited, the
plants should still prosper.*

Topdress the tray with green sphagnum
*ss. Use unchopped moss, because it may
ome established and grow naturally if
vided with sufficient moisture. This
ates an ideal environment for the plants.*

···· PLANTING SUGGESTIONS ····

Plants Used

Dionaea muscipula/summer/bog
Drosera aliciae/summer/bog
Drosera capensis 'Alba'/summer/bog
Pinguicula moranensis/summer/bog
Sarracenia species/summer/bog

Alternative Plants

Drosera rotundifolia/summer/bog
Pinguicula grandiflora/summer/bog

planting a conservatory aquarium

Aquarium plants are attractive, whether they are grown alone or arranged in an underwater garden. There are many different submerged aquatic plants from which to choose, including a wide array of foliage shapes, sizes, and colors. Among the many popular kinds are true aquatics and widely cultivated indoor terrestrial plants that adapt readily to life in an aquarium.

Although theoretically you should be able to produce a balanced ecosystem within an aquarium if only plants are present, considerable maintenance is involved in keeping an attractive display in good order, and this necessitates periodic disturbance.

Coldwater plants are easier to maintain as a viable ecosystem because their growth and development is slower, but you will still need to provide regular maintenance and ensure that the water remains clear and free from filamentous algae. When choosing plants, be su of the temperature range at which they are happiest. Ma

PLANTING AN AQUARIUM

1 Place a layer of aquarium gravel around the edge. This obscures the added compost from view.

2 Add water carefully. Pour it directly onto a plate placed on the gravel so that the compost beneath is not disturbed.

3 Install the combined pump and filter unit. This fits neatly into the corner of the aquarium and can be disguised by planti

4 Add the aquarium plants and the decorative bogwood. You can also plant lead-weighted plants into holes in the bogwood.

5 With planting complete, you can add fish. Float the bag in the water for several minutes to allow the water temperatures to equalize.

6 Switch on the pump and filter to help t ensure continued crystal clear water.

e *Vallisneria* span all the ranges,
t some sulk under cool conditions,
d they conversely become etiolated
der high temperatures and mode-
e light.

Aquarium plants are easygoing. Start
th small leafy specimens, and plant
em into a good planting compost.
ke great care when introducing the
nts to remove any snails or snail
gs because aquatic snails can wreak
voc on your garden. Plants also
nefit from the addition of carbon

Above: *A well-established aquarium, which makes good use of a wide range of aquarium plants. This ecosystem should be sustainable with careful attention.*

dioxide to the water as a fertilizer. Simple systems that can be fitted to the tank are available commercially. An example of one is illustrated on pages 58-59.

PLANTING SUGGESTIONS

Plants Used

Cryptocoryne sp./year-round/aquatic
Echinodorus paniculatus/year-round/
  aquatic
Egeria densa/year-round/aquatic
Nomophila stricta/year-round/aquatic
Vallisneria spiralis/year-round/aquatic
Vallisneria tortifolia/year-round/aquatic

Alternative Plants

Bacopa monnieri/year-round/aquatic
Hemiographis colorata/year-round/
  aquatic

making an aquascape

An aquascape could be interpreted as a landscape that exists beneath the water. Indoors it is likely to be created in an aquarium or similar glass-sided container, because it is essentially a landscaped picture viewed from the side. It is also mostly in miniature scale and can be naturally contrived or wholly artificial according to your personal taste.

Construction starts with an empty tank and a plan of where major features will be positioned. These may be rocks, ornaments, or specimen plants. Because space is limited, it is important that the positions and levels of the focal elements be determined before the rest of the aquascape is created. It is also useful to choose a printed background and to position it on the back wall of the tank at this time because it can have a considerable influence

on the positioning of the various focal elements. Various printed backgrounds are available "off the roll" at aquatic and fishkeeping outlets.

When producing an aquascape, think of it as a garden both from the construction and maintenance point of vie Make sure the planting positions retain sufficient compos to enable the plants to prosper and the plants are accessible for trimming and tidying. The surface covering of gravel or colored shells should be sufficiently deep to prevent the compost beneath from dirtying the water, bu it should not be so deep that it prevents plants from developing properly. Visually open spaces are important, so resist the temptation of crowding the aquascape and making the overall view too busy.

MAKING AN AQUASCAPE

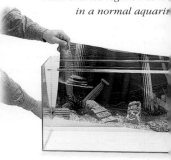

Left: An aquascape is a living aque picture, often romantic and fancifu perhaps decorated with ornaments and a printed background. Althoug it is a combination of fantasy and reality, the plants require the same maintenance regimen as the in a normal aquarit

1 *Select a suitable decorative pape background and cut it exactly to si before gluing it firmly to the outside back wall of the aquarium.*

Add aquarium compost to those areas the aquarium where you are going to plant. not run compost close to the glass sides.

3 Add decorative aquarium gravel. Pour around the edges to hide the compost and then coat the whole base of the tank.

4 Place a plate in the center of the tank and gently run water over this so that the flow does not disturb the gravel and soil.

Install the filter unit discreetly in the ner of the aquarium so that it can be den with plants or ornaments.

6 Arrange and plant the most structural plants first. Then as you add to the aquascape, step back and look at it, to ensure you are achieving the design you want.

7 Less important plants can be tucked in behind specimen plants to add depth to the leafy planting. Egeria is a good filler plant.

8 Add ornaments to complete the picture. Apart from static ornaments, you can also introduce moving ones, which attach to a pump airline. Just keep in mind that an aquascape requires regular maintenance in order to retain its quality. Regular de-leafing of the faded foliage of aquarium plants, together with the periodic scraping of the inside of the glass to prevent algae buildup, are essential.

PLANTING SUGGESTIONS

Plants Used

Alternanthera roseafolia/year-round/aquatic
Ceratopteris thalictroides/year-round/aquatic
Echinodorus paniculatus/year-round/aquatic
Egeria densa/year-round/aquatic
Hemiographis colorata/year-round/aquatic
Lysimachia nummularia 'Aurea'/year-round/ aquatic
Nomaphila stricta/year-round/aquatic
Ophiopogon 'Kyoto'/year-round/aquatic

Alternative Plants

Bacopa monnieri/year-round/aquatic
Vallisneria spiralis/year-round/aquatic

growing houseplants underwater

Gardeners who are used to cultivating houseplants in the conventional way are often surprised by the way many aquarists treat young specimens as submerged aquatics. This goes back many years when orchids like *Spiranthes* and potted plants such as the aluminum plant were used as temporary inhabitants of the aquarium. After much experimentation, now a complete range of attractive foliage plants are offered as submerged aquatics, often with different popular names.

Although such treatment of young plants may seem like sacrilege to traditional gardeners, for some plants, like the colorful-leaved *Alternanthera*, it has been their salvation. Widely grown in Victorian and Edwardian times as ground cover, this plant virtually disappeared from cultivation once this fashion was over. The discovery that they are among the most colorful and pleasing foliage plants for aquarium cultivation has secured their future, because they are now found in garden centers and pet shops everywhere.

Using houseplants as submerged plants requires careful selection. Many – such as *Spathiphyllum*, *Pilea,* and *Fittonia* – are known to adapt well to an aquatic lifestyle, and these can be introduced successfully as small plants, even if they were previously grown in the usual terrestrial fashion. Others require gradual adaptation: Golden creeping jenny, for example, is grown as a land plant with the stems trailing first into the water. Once adapted to aquatic life, the stems are removed and transplanted as an entirely submerged, but very successful, aquatic.

Above: *Pilea cadierei is also known as the aluminum plant because of its silvery marked foliage. A popular indoor foliage houseplant, it is well adapted to life underwater in the aquarium tank.*

HOUSEPLANTS UNDERWATER

1 *Houseplants that have been grown in pots should have some of their compost removed before they are planted in the gravel and compost substrate.*

2 *Introduce one or two stones to vary the terrain. This variation enables compost to be built up behind them and gives additional height.*

3 *Arrange the plants so that the aquarium appears balanced. Plants like Spathiphyllum are ideal because they form neat clumps.*

4 *Add other decorations as desired. Here black polished stones are arranged to contrast with the plain white gravel.*

5 *Once planting is complete, the plants should be carefully manicured. This includes removing any excessively tall foliage.*

6 *Place the filter unit in position. It fits neatly into the corner of the aquarium and can be disguised by the plants.*

7 *Add water, taking care not to disturb the gravel. Allow the water to run gently into a polyethylene bag, which rests on the gravel.*

8 *As the water level rises, the polyethylene bag rises with it. The bag remains in position until the aquarium is filled.*

PLANTING SUGGESTIONS

Plants Used

Dracaena hybrid/year-round/aquatic

Fittonia 'Pink Anne'/year-round/aquatic

Hypoestes hybrid/year-round/aquatic

Pilea cadierei/year-round/aquatic

Spathiphyllum hybrid (dwarf form)/ year-round/aquatic

Spathiphyllum wallisii 'Cupido'/year-round/aquatic

Alternative Plants

Chamaedorea elegans/year-round/ aquatic

Chlorophytum elatum 'Variegatum'/ year-round/aquatic

setting up a carbon dioxide fertilization system

To ensure vigorous, healthy growth of aquatic plants in an aquarium tank, a carbon dioxide fertilization system should be installed. When plant growth is unsatisfactory, especially when lighting is good and the correct growing medium is being used, then the lack of free carbon dioxide is usually the problem. Not only is carbon dioxide an important nutrient in the plants' normal daily functions and a vital element in the process of photosynthesis, a shortage of it results in poor development and growth.

In a filtered aquarium, carbon dioxide deficiency is common, and it is in such situations that a fertilization system is likely to be most necessary. In addition to facilitating plant growth, carbon dioxide prevents the precipitation of calcium dissolving in the water, thereby reducing its hardness. For this form of calcium to remain

in solution and the pH value to be stabilized, a certain amount of free carbon dioxide is necessary. This can best supplied by using a simple fertilization system, such as th one illustrated.

A typical system consists of a carbon dioxide dispensing chamber, which is attached to the side of the planted aquarium and adjusted so that the water outlet is just beneath the surface of the water. This chamber is connec to a carbon dioxide-dispensing can, which is used to char the diffusion bell with a quantity of gas. The system is fine adjusted so that a slow stream of bubbles is released into the water. Ideally, the diffusion chamber should be charge in the morning and then replenished during the day, because at night, in the absence of light, the nature of pla respiration changes, as they take in oxygen and expel carbon dioxide.

A CARBON DIOXIDE FERTILIZATION SYSTEM

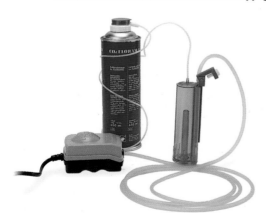

1 *A simple carbon dioxide fertilization system consists of an air pump, an airline, a diffusion bell, and a carbon dioxide gas canister. The system can be purchased complete from most aquatic suppliers.*

2 *The chamber, which includes the diffusion bell, is secured to the corner of the aquarium by a single clip. Keep in mind that the chamber should be submerged. Once installed, you can disguise the chamber with plants.*

Install the chamber once the aquarium is full of water.

3 *Once the chamber is installed, connect the carbon dioxide dispensing can. Release a little carbon dioxide in order to displace water in the diffusion bell.*

4 *The air pump is connected to the airline and carefully adjusted so that bubbles of carbon dioxide are released slowly into the tank water.*

Carbon dioxide bubbles escape through the outlet tube into the aquarium.

*The finished tank with the air pump
d carbon dioxide diffusion chamber in
sition. Bubbles of gas are released slowly
o the water during the day.*

Above: *The use of a carbon dioxide fertilization system ensures that aquatic plants enjoy vigorous and healthy growth. Even though lighting may be good and a suitable compost used, there is no guarantee that aquarium plant growth will be robust and healthy. An infusion of carbon dioxide is an enormous help.*

maintaining water clarity

Water management indoors is slightly more difficult than in cooler outdoor conditions. Changes in water clarity, especially those resulting from organic activity, are much slower in cooler temperatures. In warmth, oxygen tends to dissipate more quickly and, when fish are involved, closer attention must be paid to ensuring water movement or introducing air through an air pump.

The principles for maintaining water clarity are the same both indoors and out in that introducing liberal quantities of submerged aquatic plants helps mop up the mineral salts on which suspended algae find nourishment. Having a balanced lighting regimen and a generous population of submerged aquatic plants greatly reduces the opportunities for green water. In the described indoor features, this is an inexact science, so filters are recommended for removing organic life and debris in those settings.

Above: *Healthy plants, like this water lily,* Nymphaea *'Daubenyana,' develop when the water chemistry and soil conditions are good.*

TESTING THE WATER

1 *Take a sample of 17 oz (5 ml) of tank water, the usual amount for most tests of this type. On this occasion, a carbonate hardness test is to be conducted, but the procedure is the same for pH tests as well as other proprietary chemical tests for aquarium water. Carry out the tests every 2 weeks to check the water chemistry.*

2 *With a carbonate hardness test, one drop of reagent is added to the 17 oz (5 ml) of tank water. This turns the water blue.*

3 *More drops are added until the color changes to yellow. Multiplying the number of drops used by ten gives the carbonate hardness in milligram/liter.*

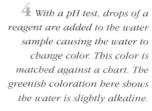

4 *With a pH test, drops of a reagent are added to the water sample causing the water to change color. This color is matched against a chart. The greenish coloration here shows the water is slightly alkaline.*

Above: *Water clarity in indoor water features needs careful monitoring because of the warmer conditions that generally prevail.*

Maintaining healthy water generally follows naturally from physical filtration. Only when fish are present in quantity need there be any serious concern over water quality. For most decorative indoor water features, fish are either undesirable or a peripheral interest.

The acidity or alkalinity of the water is only important when the measurement runs to the extremes of the scale. A periodic check with a pH test kit is simple to do, using a system rather like the litmus test in the school laboratory. There are proprietary preparations available to correct excess either way, although where conditions have gone to one extreme or the other, it is usually best to empty the water, clean the tank thoroughly, and start again.

looking after the equipment

Fortunately modern water gardening equipment is reasonably maintenance free. Pumps are now completely self-contained and only periodically require attention. Some of the smaller pumps have few components that are accessible. The larger ones that might be used with a fountain in a conservatory pool generally pull apart readily and require only a thorough washing to remove accumulated algae and organic matter.

The same applies to filters, especially in-tank filters, which benefit from regular cleaning. Undergravel filters for the most part are best left alone once they are functioning satisfactorily, particularly if plants are established above them.

Aquarium tanks benefit from periodic cleaning with a sponge scraper, which can be used to clean algae deposits from the inside walls of the tank. If you plan to keep fish in your aquarium, you should also invest in a gravel cleaner, which uses suction to suck muck and food deposits off the gravel floor of the tank where otherwise they would decompose and upset the balance of the water. Inexpensive units are available which, when primed, use a siphon effect to draw off unwanted material.

Left: The efficiency of underwater lighting is grea improved if it is regularly cleaned and accumulated slimes and algae removed.

Modern lights, like pumps, are now so well made and compact that the units more or less look after themselves It is important to clean the glass or lens regularly because algae tend to deposit an unsightly opaque coating. Where rotating or colored disc lens are attached to a pump, then regular weekly cleaning is desirable to prevent slime algae from accumulating on the lenses and fine filamentous algae from becoming entangled in the mechanism and gumming up the moving parts.

CLEANING AN AQUARIUM FILTER

Left: Disconnect the pump and filter, and separate the parts. Most modern filter assemblies are easy to pull apart. They rapidly accumulate algae and aquatic debris and should be cleaned on a regular basis.

Left: Once you dismantle the filter, clean every part of the pump and filt thoroughly using a stiff brush. Do no use a detergent because a residue this may pollute the aquarium and may prove fatal to me sensitive fish.

Many pieces of equipment can be used to maintain an aquarium. Pumps, filters, and underwater lights require regular maintenance. Other hand equipment – such as planting sticks, aquarium scrapers, and algae brushes – are all important, along with vacuum siphons for cleaning the gravel.

Below left: *A vacuum siphon or aquarium hoover sucks up aquatic debris from the floor of the tank without disturbing the plants.*

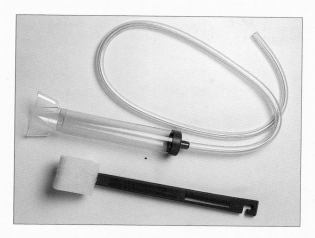

Left: *Two of the most important pieces of equipment for ensuring a clean tank are the vacuum siphon and algae brush.*

Below right: *An algae scraper or brush is used to keep the glass sides of the tank free from a buildup of algae. It is effective if used regularly.*

index

Photo Credits
Aqua Press/MP. & C. Piednoir: 5, 24, 25, 26-27, 27, 53, 59. **Eric Crichton:** 3, 8, 16 right (S. Rendell and J. Tavender, Dorset Water Lily Co, RHS Hampton Court 2001), 33 bottom left, 33 bottom right (D. Leigh, Dorset), 43 top right, 50, 61 (D. Leigh, Dorset). **John Glover:** 12 both, 20. **Jerry Harpur:** 1 (Longwood, USA), 4 (Jonathan Wheatman, NYC), 6 (Simon Fraser), 9 bottom (Luciano Giubbilei), 10 (Mark Peter Keane, Kyoto), 11 left (Ray Hudson, Johannesburg), 15 top (Little and Lewis), 15 bottom (Chris Rosmini), 17, 19 right (Luciano Giubbilei). **S. and O. Mathews:** 9 top. **Clive Nichols Garden Pictures:** 7 (Claire Mee, Candy Brothers Devt.), 11 right (Newbury Agricultural Society), 13 (Clare Matthews), 18 (Lars Hedstrom), 18-19 (Spidergarden.com, RHS Chelsea 2000), 20-21, 21 (Paul Thompson and Trevyn McDowell), 37 (Lucy Smith), 41 (Godstone Gardeners Club, RHS Chelsea 2000). **Plant Pictures World Wide:** 14-15, 16 left, 31 bottom left and right, 38 top, 56, 60. **Derek St. Romaine Photography:** 29 (Wynniatt-Husey Clarke), 35 bottom right. **Neil Sutherland:** 22, 22-23, 23 right.